AGENCY AND TRUSTS

FOR

PAYMENT OF DEBTS.

Works by the same Author.

A TREATISE

ON

THE SUCCESSION DUTY ACT.

In 12mo. Price 10s. cloth.

Shortly will be Published.

PRESCRIPTION and LIMITATION of TIME

IN RELATION TO

REAL PROPERTY

OF

THE CROWN, THE DUKE OF CORNWALL, AND PRIVATE PERSONS.

AGENCY AND TRUSTS

FOR

PAYMENT OF DEBTS

UNDER

PRIVATE ARRANGEMENT.

BY

WILLIAM BROWN, ESQ.

OF GRAY'S INN, BARRISTER-AT-LAW.

LONDON:

H. SWEET, 3, CHANCERY LANE, FLEET STREET,

Law Bookseller and Publisher.

1868.

PREFACE.

BETWEEN that class of instruments made for the discharging of debts, which, although expressing a trust in favour of the creditors, yet, in fact, create a trust, or rather a mere *agency*, in favour of the *debtor* alone, within the principle applied in the cases of *Wallwyn* v. *Coutts* (a), *Garrard* v. *Lord Lauderdale* (b) and others following them, and that class of instruments made for the like purpose creating a *trust* for the *creditors*, and not within that principle, a broad and clear distinction exists. Clear, however, as the distinction is, and easily as it may be expressed, the question, whether a given instrument made for paying the debts of the maker be one of mere agency for the debtor alone or one of trust for the creditors, is frequently difficult to determine. A case in practice involving this question led the writer to investigate the various

(a) 3 Mer. 707; 3 Sim. 14.
(b) 3 Sim. 1; 2 Russ. & M. 451.

authorities, direct and indirect, upon the subject, and the investigation suggested the possible utility, for practical purposes, of the publication of the following pages.

GRAY'S INN,
January, 1868.

CONTENTS.

CHAPTER I.

OF INSTRUMENTS IN GENERAL MADE FOR DISCHARGING THE DEBTS OF THE MAKERS.

	PAGE
1. The Kinds of Instruments to be considered	1
2. Extent of the Power of disposition of Debtors	2
3. Distinction between voluntary Settlements and Instruments for the Payment of Debts	2
4. Voluntary Conveyances as Settlements	2
5. Voluntary Conveyances in Trust to pay Creditors	3
6. Result of the Authorities as to the two Classes of Conveyances	3
7. Nature of the Distinction	4
8. How the Distinction is determined	4
9. Different Modes of making Instruments for Payment of Debts	5
10. Deeds of this Nature in Titles to Real Estate, as between Vendor and Purchaser	6

CHAPTER II.

OF INSTRUMENTS FOR THE PAYMENT OF DEBTS MADE WITHOUT THE PRIVITY OF, OR ANY COMMUNICATION WITH, ANY CREDITOR.

1. Principle of Law where Property is placed in the Hands of an Agent	8
2. Application of this Principle in relation to Instruments for Payment of Debts, but not a new Doctrine	8
3. How these Instruments are viewed	10
4. The Grounds of the Decisions of *Wallwyn* v. *Coutts* and *Garrard* v. *Lord Lauderdale*, and the Question they determined	11
5. Remarks on the Extent to which the Doctrine has been applied	13

		PAGE
6. Revocability of these Instruments as to Creditors	..	14
7. Revocability of these Instruments as between the Parties not Creditors	..	15
8. Operation against an Execution, and until assented to	.	16
9. Effect of the Trustee acting	..	16
10. Effect of the Death of the Maker	..	16
11. When the Operation is at the Will of the Debtor	..	17
12. Effect of the Instrument as a Conversion, in Equity, of Real Estate	..	17
13. Nature of the Instrument as respects Surplus after Creditors entitled are satisfied	..	17
14. Effect when part of a Family Arrangement	..	18
15. Requirements from Creditors to entitle them to the Benefits	..	19
16. Applicability of the Doctrine where Creditors take after the Debtor's Death, and the Lands charged are conveyed as Bounty to a third Person	..	19
17. How long the Instrument continues revocable	..	20
18. Revocability as respects the legal Estate	..	20
19. Authorities consistent with those on voluntary Settlements, and Contracts giving Rights to third Persons not Parties	..	21
20. Allowances to the Trustee or Agent and his Equity, as to his obligations for the Debtor, before a Re-conveyance	..	22
21. Creditors expressed to be, but not Parties	..	22
22. Instruments of the nature of those here considered, and also of those the subject of the next Chapter	..	22

CHAPTER III.

OF INSTRUMENTS FOR THE PAYMENT OF DEBTS MADE WITH THE PRIVITY OF, OR ON COMMUNICATION WITH, THE CREDITORS.

1. Voluntary Conveyances	..	23
2. Instruments for the Payment of Debts distinguishable from such Conveyances	..	23

		PAGE
3. The Instruments considered here and those in the last Chapter differ, and how the privity of, or the communication with, the Creditors appears		24
4. When made to a Creditor		26
5. When so made but not for securing a Debt		28
6. When the Creditors should come in and execute the Instrument		28
7. Debtor covenanting to surrender, but not surrendering a Trustee		29
8. Instruments made by way of Security		29
9. With an express Power of Revocation		30
10. One Creditor may sue for all		30
11. Instruments irrevocable in part, and revocable in other part if in a separate Instrument, whether irrevocable *in toto*		30

CHAPTER IV.

OF INSTRUMENTS FOR THE PAYMENT OF DEBTS MADE WITHOUT THE PRIVITY OF, BUT AFTERWARDS COMMUNICATED TO, AND ASSENTED TO OR ADOPTED BY, THE CREDITORS.

SECT. I.—*Of the communication of the Instrument to, or the adoption of or the assent to it by, the Creditors.*

1. Questions as to Creditors not executing, but apprized of the Execution of the Instrument, becoming *cestui que trust*	34
2. Execution of the Instrument by the Creditors not necessary	34
3. What necessary to give Creditors the benefit of the Instrument	34
4. Notice of it by the Debtor to the Creditor	35
5. Whether the mere communication of it to the Creditors be sufficient to give them the benefit of it	36
6. Creditor a Party to and executing the Deed	39
7. Communication of it to be charged in Bill	39
8. Instrument made without the privity of, and not afterwards communicated to or adopted by, the Creditors, *Synnot* v. *Simpson*	39

CONTENTS.

SECT. II.—*How and when the assent to, or the adoption of, the Instrument may be signified.*

	PAGE
1. Assent, what	42
2. Assent by the Persons named as Trustees	43
3. Assent or adoption by the Creditors	43
4, 5. By the Creditors acting on the Instrument	44
6. Receipt of Interest by thém from the Debtors	44
7. Assent, when to be given	45
8. Creditors assenting within a time limited, whether affected by those assenting afterwards	45
9. Assent after the death of the Debtor, when ineffectual	46
10. Refusal not retracted	46
11. Whether assent implied after withdrawal of express dissent	46
12. The object of these Instruments, and how the benefits of them may be lost	46
13. Creditor after Notice seeking payment of his Debt from another source, or not retracting a refusal	47

SECT. III.—*The Effect of the communication, and of assent or adoption.*

1. Instrument revocable until communicated to or adopted by the Creditors	47
2. After communication, assent or adoption, irrevocable	48
3. The Trusts express and not affected by lapse of time between the Trustee and the Creditors	48
4. Trust also in the cases furnishing the principle of the Decisions on these Instruments, but constructive or *quasi* only; and when, and when not, within the Statute of Limitations, 21 Jac. 1, c. 16	48
5. Creditors not suing the Debtor on the faith of the Instrument protected in a suit impeaching the Instrument	49

TABLE OF CASES CITED.

A.
	PAGE
Acton v. Woodgate	9, 16, 21, 27, 31, 36, 38, 48

B.
Baron v. Husband	8
Bill v. Cureton	3, 21
Broadbent v. Thornton	45
Browne v. Cavendish	2, 36, 37

C.
Collins v. Reece	45
Colyear v. The Countess of Mulgrave	18
Cornthwaite v. Frith	9, 35
Cosser v. Radford	5, 35, 44
Crawford v. Crawford	49

D.
Donegal, Marquis of v. Grey	21
Drever v. Mawdesley	9, 18, 19, 22
Dudgeon v. O'Connell	45
Dunch v. Kent	45

E.
Ellison v. Ellison	3, 21
Evans v. Bagwell	9, 17, 34, 35

F.
Field v. Lord Donoughmore	29, 34, 47
Fitzgerald v. Stewart	8, 16, 35, 42, 49
Foley v. Hoare	9

xii   TABLE OF CASES CITED.

Foley v. Hill	49
Forbes v. Limond	44
Fortescue v. Barnett	3, 21
Foster v. Blackstone	9

G.

Garrard v. Lord Lauderdale	v, 8, 9, 10, 11, 12, 14, 20, 21, 25, 26, 35, 36, 37, 47
Gaskell v. Gaskell	8, 16
Gibbs v. Glamis	9
Gould v. Robertson	45
Grant v. Austen	35
Gray v. Knox	21
Greene v. Stoney	18
Gresty v. Gibson	25
Griffith v. Ricketts	3, 4, 5, 17, 18, 24, 27, 30, 32, 36, 37, 48
Gurney v. Lord Oranmore	24, 26

H.

Harland v. Binks	9, 34, 38, 42, 43, 48
Heath v. Henley	49
Hill v. Secretan	8
Hollis' (Lord) case	49
Holmes v. Love	45
Hughes v. Stubbs	5
Hunt v. Jessel	27
Hutchinson v. Heyworth	38

J.

Johnson v. Kershaw	46, 47

K.

Kirwan v. Daniel	8, 9, 16, 35, 37, 42

L.

Lancaster v. Elce	25
Lane v. Husband	34, 46
Latouche v. Earl of Lucan	9, 12, 35

TABLE OF CASES CITED.

	PAGE
Lett v. Morris	35
Lewis v. Jones	45
Lilly v. Hays	38, 48

M.

M'Donnell v. Hesilrige	3
Mackinnon v. Stewart	5, 8, 12, 15, 20, 25, 26, 28, 29, 34, 36
Montefiore v. Browne	6, 21, 24, 30, 31, 36, 38, 39
Morrell v. Wootten	8, 9, 16, 34, 35

N.

Nicholson v. Tutin	35, 45
Noble v. National Discount Company	48

O.

Ord and Barber v. Union Bank of Scotland	8

P.

Page v. Broom	9
Paterson v. Murphy	3, 21
Petre v. Espinasse	3
Pulvertoft v. Pulvertoft	3, 21
Pye, Ex parte	3, 21

R.

Ravenshaw v. Hollier	9, 18
Reeves v. Watts	25
Rowe v. Dawson	34

S.

Scott v. Porcher	8, 16, 20, 35, 49
Sheldon v. Weldman	49
Siggers v. Evans	9, 14, 15, 16, 27, 39, 42, 43, 44
Simmonds v. Palles	5, 9, 14
Slade v. Rigg	9
Small v. Marwood	43, 45
Smith v. Clay	49
—— v. Garland	3, 21

TABLE OF CASES CITED.

	PAGE
Smith v. Hurst..	2, 4, 5, 15, 28, 50
—— v. Keating	9, 15, 38, 48
—— v. Pococke	49
South, Ex parte	34
Spooner v. Whiston	45
Spottiswoode v. Stockdale	34, 45
Squire v. Ford	24, 30
Steele v. Murphy	9, 21
Stoughton v. Crosbie	21
Synnot v. Simpson	2, 6, 9, 12, 13, 14, 16, 18, 19, 21, 22, 24, 29, 30, 31, 35, 39, 42, 45

T.

Tatlock v. Smith	45
Taylor v. Stibbert	21
Teed v. Beere	49
Townshend v. Townshend	48

W.

Walker v. Rostron	48
Wallwyn v. Coutts	v, 8, 10, 11, 14, 26, 32
Wedderburn v. Wedderburn	48
Wedlake v. Hurley	8, 35
Wilding v. Richards	3, 5, 9, 11, 16, 17, 21, 22, 24, 29, 32, 36, 48
Williams v. Everett	8, 16, 20, 35, 42, 43
—— v. Mostyn	45

Y.

Yates v. Bell	35

AGENCY AND TRUSTS

FOR

PAYMENT OF DEBTS.

CHAPTER I.

OF INSTRUMENTS IN GENERAL MADE FOR DISCHARGING THE DEBTS OF THE MAKERS.

1. *The Kinds of Instruments to be considered.*
2. *Extent of the Power of disposition of Debtors.*
3. *Distinction between voluntary Settlements and Instruments for the Payment of Debts.*
4. *Voluntary Conveyances as Settlements.*
5. *Voluntary Conveyances in Trust to pay Creditors.*
6. *Result of the Authorities as to the two Classes of Conveyances.*
7. *Nature of the Distinction.*
8. *How the Distinction is determined.*
9. *Different Modes of making Instruments for Payment of Debts.*
10. *Deeds of this Nature in Titles to Real Estate, as between Vendor and Purchaser.*

1. THE instruments which are here the subject of consideration do not embrace those which are made under, or in pursuance of, or in connection with, the laws of bankruptcy or of insolvency, or any arrangement under those laws between debtors and their creditors, or of or with any other statute, but embrace only those

instruments so frequently made by debtors for discharging their debts, exclusive of those laws and any other statute, by way of mere private arrangement, either independent of, or between them and their creditors.

2. Subject to the statutory rights in case of bankruptcy or insolvency, and other statutory remedies, every debtor has, according to the law of this country, a perfect right to deal with his property in any mode which he may think best, provided he acts honestly in the disposal of it. He may dispose of it in favour of all or of any one or more of his creditors; and the law does not interfere with his power and right to do so, if it be exercised *bonâ fide* (*a*).

3. It is important to keep in view the distinction between voluntary settlements and conveyances upon trust to pay creditors: for they run so much into each other that it is hard, in all cases, to draw the line between them. In the former the relation of trustee and *cestui que trust* is, but in the latter is not, created. Properly speaking the creditors are not in the position of and are considered as not intended to be *cestuis que trust* (*b*).

4. A voluntary conveyance of property to trustees upon trust for a third party when the trust is executed, as distinguished from a trust merely executory, may create an indefeasible trust in favour of that party (*c*).

(*a*) *Smith* v. *Hurst*, 10 Hare, 30.
(*b*) *Browne* v. *Cavendish*, 1 Jo. & Lat. 606; *Synnot* v. *Simpson*, 5 H. L. C. 121, 145.
(*c*) *Ellison* v. *Ellison*, 6 Ves. 656; *Pulvertoft* v. *Pulvertoft*, 18 Ib. 84; *Ex parte Pye*, Ib. 140; *Smith* v. *Garland*, 2 Mer. 123; *Bill* v. *Cureton*, 2 Myl. & K. 503; *Petre* v. *Espinasse*, Ib.

5. On the other hand, a conveyance of property upon trust to pay creditors not parties to the transaction has been very reasonably held to create a trust for the author of the deed, and not for his creditors. Such an instrument, though in form a deed of trust, may have been intended to be an instrument, in effect, of agency—a mere direction to a person in the situation of steward or agent, or in an analogous position, as to the mode of distributing or applying the property of the person executing the deed, without any intention on his part of creating in any other person a right against it. In which simple case it is clear that the debtor may countermand the authority, unless the agent has acted upon it, so as to give the creditors an interest in the money in his hands (*d*). It is established that in such cases, if the Court, having the deed before it, is satisfied that the intention was so, the intention is to have effect given to it, though in form the deed be a deed of trust (*e*).

6. The result of the cases upon these two kinds of deeds appears to be this: in cases of deeds vesting property in trustees upon trust for the benefit of particular persons, the deed cannot be revoked, altered or modified by the party who has created the trust; but in cases of deeds purporting to be executed for the benefit of creditors, the question whether the trust can

---

502; *Fortescue* v. *Barnett*, 3 Ib. 36; *Paterson* v. *Murphy*, 11 Hare, 88; *Griffith* v. *Ricketts*, 7 Hare, 299; *McDonnell* v. *Hesilrige*, 16 Beav. 346.

(*d*) See *Griffith* v. *Ricketts*, 7 Hare, 299, 308; *Wilding* v. *Richards*, 1 Coll. 655.

(*e*) *Wilding* v. *Richards*, *supra*.

be revoked, altered or modified depends upon the circumstances of each particular case. It is difficult at first sight to see the distinction between the two classes of cases, for in each of the classes a trust is purported to be created, and the property is vested in the trustees; but the distinction appears to be in this:—In cases of trust for the benefit of particular persons, the party creating the trust can have no other object than to benefit the persons in whose favour the trust is created, and, the trust being well created, the property, in equity, belongs to the *cestuis que trust* as much as it would belong to them at law, if the legal interest had been transferred to them; but in cases of deeds purporting to be executed for the benefit of creditors, and to which no creditor is a party, the motive of the party executing the deed may have been either to benefit his creditors or to promote his own convenience (*f*).

7. The distinction between these two classes of decisions is, said Sir C. Pepys, M. R. (*g*), somewhat refined, but has obviously good sense for its foundation; and the rule, as established by them, is adopted to promote the views and intentions of the parties.

8. Although, however, this distinction in principle is marked and obvious, yet to decide to which of the two classes of cases a given instrument belongs is often a task of difficulty (*h*). Whether an instrument be one of trust or of mere agency only is a question of intention. It is not rendered necessary by the authorities on this

(*f*) *Smith* v. *Hurst*, 10 Hare, 30.
(*g*) 2 Myl. & K. 511.
(*h*) *Griffith* v. *Ricketts*, 7 Hare, 299.

subject to say, that every deed in favour of creditors to which no creditor is a party, is an instrument of the latter description. The court looks into and determines from the nature of the transaction what the effect of it shall be in divesting the owner of the property to which it relates, and in each case must be guided by the particular circumstances (*i*). To determine to which of the two classes of cases a given trust deed belongs depends upon the intention of the author of the deed, to be collected from the deed itself and such surrounding circumstances as may be admissible in aid of the interpretation of the deed (*k*). The motive of the party executing the deed may have been either to benefit his creditors, or to promote his own convenience; and the court has there to examine into the circumstances for the purpose of ascertaining what was the true purpose of the deed; and this examination does not stop with the deed itself, but must be carried on to what has subsequently occurred, because the party who has created the trust may, by his own conduct, or by the obligations which he has permitted his trustee to contract, have created an equity against himself (*l*).

9. An instrument may be made by a debtor for the payment of his debts generally, or of a specific class

(*i*) *Hughes* v. *Stubbs*, 1 Hare, 476, 479; *Griffith* v. *Ricketts*, 7 Ib. 299; *Mackinnon* v. *Stewart*, 1 Sim. N. S. 80; *Wilding* v. *Richards*, 1 Coll. 661; *Cosser* v. *Radford*, 1 De G. J. & S. 585; *Simmonds* v. *Palles*, 2 Jo. & Lat. 489.

(*k*) *Griffith* v. *Ricketts*, 7 Hare, 299; *Wilding* v. *Richards*, 1 Coll. 661; *Smith* v. *Hurst*, 10 Hare, 30; *Synnot* v. *Simpson*, 5 H. L. C. 121.

(*l*) *Per* Turner, V.-C., *Smith* v. *Hurst*, 10 Hare, 30, 47.

of debts, or of a debt or debts specifically mentioned, and either without the privity of, or any communication with, any creditor, or with the privity of some creditor or creditors, or as to some creditors without, and as to others with, such privity, or without the privity of, but afterwards communicated to and adopted by, some creditor or creditors; and in any case, either with or without such creditor or creditors being parties, either formal or actual, to the instrument.

10. Deeds of this nature are frequently found in titles to real estates, and, between vendor and purchaser, require great vigilance on the part of the latter, who ought most carefully to guard against assuming too hastily that, as respects the payment of the debts, the deed is a mere instrument of agency, and revocable at the will of the debtor. The necessity for this vigilance is strongly illustrated by two very recent decisions in the House of Lords (*m*). The latter case is not so strong as the former one; for in the latter the creditor was a party to and executed the instrument, whereas in the former the creditor was neither party nor privy to it. Even where an express power of revocation is reserved to two or more debtors jointly to which a trust to pay debts may be subject, yet on the death of one of them the power may be no longer exercisable, and the trust will become absolute, as in the latter of these two cases. These two cases will repay a careful perusal and consideration, especially the judgment of Lord St. Leonards, in the former case, who differed from the rest of the Court.

(*m*) *Synnot* v. *Simpson*, 5 H. L. C. 121; *Montefiore* v. *Browne*, 7 Ib. 241.

CHAPTER II.

OF INSTRUMENTS FOR THE PAYMENT OF DEBTS MADE WITHOUT THE PRIVITY OF, OR ANY COMMUNICATION WITH, ANY CREDITOR.

1. *Principle of Law where Property is placed in the Hands of an Agent.*
2. *Application of this Principle in relation to Instruments for Payment of Debts, but not a new Doctrine.*
3. *How these Instruments are viewed.*
4. *The Grounds of the Decisions of* Wallwyn *v.* Coutts *and* Garrard *v.* Lord Lauderdale, *and the Question they determined.*
5. *Remarks on the Extent to which the Doctrine has been applied.*
6. *Revocability of these Instruments as to Creditors.*
7. *Revocability of these Instruments as between the Parties not Creditors.*
8. *Operation against an Execution, and until assented to.*
9. *Effect of the Trustee acting.*
10. *Effect of the Death of the Maker.*
11. *When the Operation is at the Will of the Debtor.*
12. *Effect of the Instrument as a Conversion, in Equity, of Real Estate.*
13. *Nature of the Instrument as respects Surplus after Creditors entitled are satisfied.*
14. *Effect when part of a Family Arrangement.*
15. *Requirements from Creditors to entitle them to the Benefits.*
16 *Applicability of the Doctrine where Creditors take after the Debtor's Death, and the Lands charged are conveyed as Bounty to a third Person.*
17. *How long the Instrument continues revocable.*
18. *Revocability as respects the legal Estate.*

19. *Authorities consistent with those on voluntary Settlements, and Contracts giving Rights to third Persons not Parties.*
20. *Allowances to the Trustee or Agent and his Equity, as to his obligations for the Debtor, before a Re-conveyance.*
21. *Creditors expressed to be, but not Parties.*
22. *Instruments of the nature of those here considered, and also of those the subject of the next Chapter.*

———

1. ANY person, not being under any personal incapacity or disability, may make another person his agent or attorney to get in his property, and to distribute it amongst his creditors, or in any other mode he may direct (*a*); and has a right to countermand and revoke the destination of the property, as being merely in the hands of his agent or mandatory, until some right has been created in the parties who were to benefit by the distribution (*b*).

2. This principle has been applied to certain instruments made for the benefit of creditors, the subject of this chapter, and was first recognized and acted upon in the case of *Wallwyn* v. *Coutts* (*c*), which was followed in *Garrard* v. *Lord Lauderdale* (*d*), has been

---

(*a*) *Mackinnon* v. *Stewart*, 1 Sim. N. S. 80, 89.
(*b*) See *Hill* v. *Secretan*, 1 Bos. & P. 315; *Williams* v. *Everett*, 14 East, 582; *Scott* v. *Porcher*, 3 Mer. 652; *Garrard* v. *Lord Lauderdale*, 2 Russ. & M. 451, 455; *Fitzgerald* v. *Stewart*, 2 Sim. 333; 2 Russ. & M. 457, *S. C.* on appeal; *Kirwan* v. *Daniel*, 5 Hare, 493; *Wedlake* v. *Hurley*, 1 C. & J. 83; *Baron* v. *Husband*, 4 B. & Ad. 611; *Ord & Barber* v. *Union Bank of Scotland*, 1 Macq. 513; *Gaskell* v. *Gaskell*, 2 You. & J. 502; *Morrell* v. *Wootten*, 16 Beav. 197.
(*c*) 3 Mer. 707; misreported there, 5 Hare, 499; again reported, 3 Sim. 14.
(*d*) 3 Sim. 1.

considered as established by the former case, and appears to have been acted upon ever since; not that it was new law, but brought directly into operation by that case (*e*). In the latter of these two cases the creditors were named as parties to the deed, of the third part; the trustees gave notice of the deed to the creditors (of whom the plaintiff was one) who were parties of the third part, and the Court held that the notice was immaterial. The case to that extent has been said to be a case of the first impression, and the decision a surprise on those in whose favour it was pronounced (*f*).

These two cases are the leading authorities on the subject, and the principle upon which they are founded has been enunciated and applied in numerous other cases arising upon instruments of this nature, both in equity (*g*) and at law (*h*), as an established principle.

In *Garrard* v. *Lord Lauderdale*(*i*) Shadwell,

(*e*) *La Touche* v. *Earl of Lucan*, 1 West, H. L. C. 477; 7 Cl. & F. 772, *S.C.*

(*f*) *Per* Wigram, V.-C., *Kirwan* v. *Daniel*, 5 Hare, 493, 499.

(*g*) *Foster* v. *Blackstone*, 1 Myl. & K. 297; *Acton* v. *Woodgate*, 2 Ib. 494; *Gibbs* v. *Glamis*, 11 Sim. 584, 591; *Steele* v. *Murphy*, 3 M. P. C. C. 445; *Drever* v. *Mawdesley*, 16 Sim. 511; *Simmonds* v. *Palles*, 2 Jo. & Lat. 489; *Evans* v. *Bagwell*, 2 Con. & L. 612; *Page* v. *Broom*, 4 Russ. 6; *Slade* v. *Rigg*, 3 Hare, 35; *La Touche* v. *Earl of Lucan*, 2 Dru. & Wal. 432; 1 West, H. L. C. 477; 7 Cl. & F. 772, *S.C.*; *Cornthwaite* v. *Frith*, 5 De G. & S. 550; *Synnot* v. *Simpson*, 5 H. L. C. 121; *Ravenshaw* v. *Hollier*, 7 Sim. 3; *Foley* v. *Hoare*, Hayes & J. Ir. Rep. 90; *Wilding* v. *Richards*, 1 Coll. 655; *Morrell* v. *Wootten*, 16 Beav. 197.

(*h*) *Harland* v. *Binks*, 15 Q. B. 713; *Smith* v. *Keating*, 6 C. B. 136; *Siggers* v. *Evans*, 5 Ell. & B. 367.

(*i*) 8 Sim. 1, 12.

V.-C., said he apprehended that Lord Eldon must have considered that where a person does, without the privity of any one, without receiving any consideration, and without notice to any creditor, himself make a disposition, as between himself and trustees, for the payment of his debts, he is merely directing the mode in which his own property shall be applied for his own benefit, and that the general creditors or the creditors named in the schedule are merely persons named there for the purpose of showing how the trust property under the voluntary deed shall be applied for the benefit of the volunteers (*j*). And in the same case on appeal Lord Brougham, C., said he doubted the accuracy of the report of *Wallwyn* v. *Coutts*, where Lord Eldon is represented to have said, he refused the motion on the ground of the trust being voluntary, and consequently a trust which could not be enforced against the Duke of Marlborough and his son the Marquess (*k*).

3. These instruments, although in form and terms deeds of trust, are, as between the debtor and the trustees, except where one or more of the trustees may be a creditor or creditors, as will be seen in the next chapter, voluntary, that is without valuable consideration, and being, as between the trustees and the creditors, executory only, without creating between them the relation of trustee and *cestui que trusts* (*l*), are not available by the creditors, but are viewed, both at law and in equity, as simple transactions between an

(*j*) 5 Ell. & B. 378.
(*k*) 2 Russ. & M. 453.
(*l*) See *Garrard* v. *Lord Lauderdale*.

agent and his principal, and governed by the principle just stated (*m*). The debtor is regarded as the principal, and the person to whom the deed is made as the agent of the debtor. On the appeal in *Garrard* v. *Lord Lauderdale*, Lord Brougham, C., said (*n*) the real nature of the deed is, not so much a conveyance vesting a trust in A. for the benefit of the creditors of the grantor; but rather that it may be likened to an arrangement made by a debtor for his own personal convenience and accommodation—for payment of his own debts in an order prescribed by himself—over which he retains power and control, and with respect to which the creditors can have no right to complain, inasmuch as they are not injured by it, they waive no right of action, and are not executing parties to it.

4. The cases *Wallwyn* v. *Coutts* and *Garrard* v. *Lord Lauderdale*, said Sir C. Pepys, M. R. (*o*), so far from deciding that a *cestui que trust* becoming entitled under a voluntary settlement had not a good title against the settlor, proceeded upon this, that the character of trustee and *cestui que trust* never existed between the creditor and the trustees of the trust deeds, but that the settlor was the only *cestui que trust*, and therefore that he was entitled to direct the application of his own trust fund. . . . . His Honor, after saying he did not wish to have it supposed that he entertained any doubt of the propriety of those decisions, added that the distinction between them and the prior cases is somewhat refined, is true; but it is obvious that the

(*m*) *Wilding* v. *Richards*, 1 Coll. 661.
(*n*) 2 Russ. & M. 451, 455.
(*o*) 2 Myl. & K. 511.

distinction has good sense for its foundation, and that the rule, as established by them, is adopted to promote the views and intentions of the parties. A man who, without any communication with his creditors, puts property into the hands of trustees for the purpose of paying his debts, proposes only a benefit to himself by the payment of his debts—his object is not to benefit his creditors: it would therefore be a result most remote from the contemplation of the debtor, if it should be held that any creditor discovering the transaction should be able to fasten upon the property and invest himself with the character of *cestui que trust* (p). What was really decided in *Garrard* v. *Lord Lauderdale* and other cases involving the same point, was only this: that in such a case the conveyance of property to the agent makes no difference as to the right of revocation in the debtor. The party in whom the property has been vested is a mere trustee for the debtor, by whom it has been conveyed to him. He is still the mere agent or attorney of the debtor, and must obey his directions as to the disposal of the property (q).

These cases have proceeded on the principle that where a person who is indebted makes provision for payment of his debts by vesting property in trustees for the purpose of discharging them, but does so behind the backs of the creditors, and without communicating with them, the trustees do not become trustees for the creditors. The arrangement is one supposed to be made by the debtor for his own convenience only; it

(p) *La Touche* v. *The Earl of Lucan*, 7 Cl. & F. 772; 1 West, 477, S. C. See also *Synnot* v. *Simpson*, 5 H. L. C. 121, 151.

(q) *Mackinnon* v. *Stewart*, 1 Sim. N. S. 80, 89.

is as if he had put a sum of money into the hands of an agent with directions to apply it in paying certain specified debts. In such a case there is no privity between the agent and the creditor. The debtor may at any time revoke the authority given to his agent and may recall the money placed in his hands. The agent is the agent exclusively of the debtor, not of the creditor. No action could be maintained against him by the creditor; there is no privity between them. The same principle precisely applies where the debtor, instead of placing money in the hands of another with directions to apply it in discharge of his debts conveys real estate to him in order to its being converted into money by sale or mortgage, so that the money raised may be applied in discharge of debts. The person in whom real estate is so vested is a trustee, not for the creditor, but for the debtor. When in pursuance of his trust the trustee sells and pays the debtor his demand, he does so in pursuance of the directions given to him by his principal, the debtor, from whom he received the property, not in discharge of any duty which he owes to the creditor: the debtor is alone the person to whom the trustee is to look. The debtor may regulate the disposition of the property as he thinks fit; may order the proceeds of it to be applied in discharge of his debts, and may then revoke these orders and give fresh directions without regard to the interests of those for whose benefit the prior orders would have operated (*r*).

5. The extent to which the doctrine of these cases has been applied, has been the subject of remark and

(*r*) *Synnot* v. *Simpson*, 5 H. L. C. 121, 138.

not always of entire approval. There is no doubt, said Lord St. Leonards (*s*), that the doctrine in *Wallwyn* v. *Coutts* and *Garrard* v. *Lord Lauderdale* has gone creeping on to an extent not intended by those who laid down the rule; and he afterwards said (*t*) those cases had certainly gone a great length, he was not disposed to carry the principle further than authority compelled him, and he was never quite reconciled to the authorities. He submitted to them but would not carry them further (*u*). But he remarked that it might be said in favour of the doctrine, carried to the extent it has been, that it would be inconvenient if a creditor, hearing of such a deed, to which he was not a party, could, in half an hour after it was signed, file a bill to have the trust executed (*x*). He thought, however, the decisions both convenient and very just, as enabling the parties to make arrangements for paying claims which may afterwards arise as between themselves (*y*).

6. So long as deeds of this class are not adopted or assented to by the creditor or creditors whose debt or debts are to be paid, they are simply mandatory (*z*), and taken alone and without reference to the trustee or some of the trustees being a creditor or creditors of the maker, and to the dealings with other creditors, are mere deeds of management which it is competent for

(*s*) 2 Con. & L. 616.
(*t*) *Simmonds* v. *Palles*, 2 Jo. & Lat. 489, 495, 504.
(*u*) See also *Synnot* v. *Simpson*, 5 H. L. C. 121, 148, 150.
(*x*) 2 Con. & L. 616.
(*y*) 5 H. L. C. 153.
(*z*) *Siggers* v. *Evans*, 5 Ell. & B. 367.

him at any time to alter or revoke, and cannot be permitted to be set up against creditors but is fraudulent against them. A deed which the debtor has power to revoke, and attempts to use as a shield against his creditors, cannot be otherwise than fraudulent and void against the creditors (*a*). The conveyance of the property to the agent makes no difference as to the right of revocation in the debtor (*b*), and although the person to whom the deed is made assent to it, it has no operation at law to pass the property as against an execution until a trust has been created in favour of the creditor or creditors (*c*), and is revocable by the insolvency of the debtor (*d*).

7. But when the instrument is made by two co-owners of the property, although the deed may still remain, as respects the creditors, revocable, yet it may not be revocable by the surviving owner to the injury of the estate of the deceased owner. The death does not vary the case as to the creditors. The revocability of the trust for the creditors is a consequence of its not being binding on the parties creating it. But the revocability by the survivor of such owners, to the injury of the estate of the deceased owner is not a necessary consequence, and does not give a right to the creditors which up to that moment they did not possess. If the trust be originally one of which, though

(*a*) *Smith* v. *Hurst*, 10 Hare, 30; *Siggers* v. *Evans, supra; Smith* v. *Keating*, 6 C. B. 136, in Cam. Scacc.
(*b*) *Mackinnon* v. *Stewart*, 1 Sim. N. S. 80, 89.
(*c*) *Siggers* v. *Evans, supra*.
(*d*) See *Smith* v. *Keating, supra*.

they may reap the benefit, they cannot enforce the execution, a shifting right of the owners, as between themselves, cannot give to the creditors a claim, which under the contract, as it stood originally, the law would deny to them (*d*).

8. Although the person to whom the deed is made assent to it, yet it has no operation to pass the property as against an execution (*e*), and cannot be enforced by any creditor until a trust has been raised for him (*f*), or until such person has assented to it in a way to create the relation of trustee and *cestui que trust* (*g*).

9. The instrument in form may be in strict conformity with the intention of the parties, but, as respects the creditors intended to be benefited, the mere circumstance of the trustee taking upon himself to act under the instrument, without creating any right in them, will not impart to the deed any operation for their benefit (*h*).

10. The death of the maker of the instrument, although preventing the actual revocation or recall,

---

(*d*) See the judgment of Lord St. Leonards, *Synnot* v. *Simpson*, 5 H. L. C. 121, 145.

(*e*) See *Siggers* v. *Evans*, 5 Ell. & B. 367, 376.

(*f*) See *Williams* v. *Everett*, 14 East, 582.

(*g*) Ib.; *Scott* v. *Porcher*, 3 Mer. 652; *Fitzgerald* v. *Stewart*, 2 Sim. 233; 2 Russ. & M. 457; *Kirwan* v. *Daniel*, 5 Hare, 493; *Morrell* v. *Wootten*, 16 Beav. 197; *Gaskell* v. *Gaskell*, 2 You. & J. 502.

(*h*) See *Acton* v. *Woodgate*, 2 Myl. & K. 494; *Wilding* v. *Richards*, 1 Coll. 655.

does not alter either the character or the effect of the instrument (*i*).

11. If the instrument be express or imply that the provisions of it for the benefit of the creditors shall not be available without the consent of the debtor, and the instrument be not communicated to or acted upon by the creditors claiming the benefit of the deed, they cannot enforce it (*k*).

12. The instrument, however, apart from its primary object, may effect, in equity, from the time it is made, an absolute conversion of any real estate comprised in it into personalty, and may divert the current of the devolution of the property, divesting the real representatives of the grantor of their title to the estate and the proceeds of the conversion, and vesting the estate so constructively converted as personalty in his personal representatives, although the recall or the revocation of the deed by the grantor, without any actual reconveyance to him by the grantees, may operate to reconvert the property and to restore the original current of devolution. But even if the instrument make no such diversion, the effect of the conversion may still be to vest the property in the real representatives as personal estate (*l*).

13. Sometimes a question may arise whether an instrument of this nature, as respects any surplus remain-

---

(*i*) *Wilding* v. *Richards*, 1 Coll. 655; *Griffith* v. *Ricketts*, 7 Hare, 299.
(*k*) *Evans* v. *Bagwell*, 2 Con. & L. 612.
(*l*) See *Griffith* v. *Ricketts*, 7 Hare, 299, and cases cited.

ing after satisfying the debt or debts of the creditor or creditors who have acquired an interest under the instrument, still retains its mandatory character, and be therefore revocable. In *Griffiths* v. *Ricketts* (m) this question was raised but was not necessary to be decided, and the Court said it was not prepared to decide the question in the affirmative.

14. Provisions for the payment of debts are frequently found in deeds of family arrangement, forming, as between members of a family, part of a contract between them, or some of them, and founded on a valuable consideration. The entire arrangement is between themselves only, and the right to enforce it is reciprocal, and yet none of the creditors whose debts are to be paid, who are not parties to the deed, with whom there has been no contract, none of whose rights or remedies have been prejudiced by the deed, and who have not acted upon it, can enforce the payment of their debts by the trustees (n).

When two persons for valuable consideration between themselves covenant to do some act for the benefit of a mere stranger, that stranger has no right to enforce the covenant against the two, although each one might against the other (o). The question, however, whether in such cases any trust in favour of the creditors, or only a mere agency is created, is, as we have already seen (p), one of intention, and in

(m) 7 Hare, 299.
(n) See *Ravensham* v. *Hollier*, 7 Sim. 3; *Synnot* v. *Simpson*, 5 H. L. C. 121; *Greene* v. *Stoney*, 13 Ir. Eq. Rep. 801; *Drever* v. *Mawdesley*, 16 Sim. 511.
(o) See *Colyear* v. *The Countess of Mulgrave*, 2 Keen, 81, 98.
(p) *Ante*, pp. 4, 5.

determining the question much difficulty will be often experienced, as is shown by the case of *Synnot* v. *Simpson* in the House of Lords, particularly noticed hereafter, where it was held, affirming the judgment of the Court below, Lord St. Leonards *dissentiente*, that such a trust was created.

15. In instruments of this nature the creditors may be required, in order to entitle themselves to the benefits of them, to submit to the uncontrolled judgment and discretion of the trustees, not only the amount of their debts but all the circumstances attending them, but also that the trustees should take into consideration not merely what appertains to the creditors in respect of their debts, but also what may be the probable situation of the debtor, in the event of the trustees not making any arrangement satisfactory to the creditors (*q*).

16. Lord Cranworth, in *Synnot* v. *Simpson* (*r*), doubted whether, where the trust is to come into operation only on the death of its author, as he thought it was there, and where, subject to the trust for payment of debts, the lands charged are conveyed by way of bounty to a third person, the doctrine of *Garrard* v. *Lord Lauderdale* and in the other authorities applied, and thought it, at all events, open to argument that in such a case the settlor must, *primâ facie*, be understood to be dealing with his property as if he was disposing of it by will, and therefore as contemplating bounty throughout; or, if it be contract, so far as the party taking the estate is concerned, that it must still

(*q*) See *Drever* v. *Mawdesley*, 16 Sim. 511.
(*r*) 5 H. L. C. 121.

be considered as bounty in favour of the incumbrancers; admitting, however, that in each case the question was one of construction. But Lord St. Leonards thought it was not the fact that in the case before the Court the trust was not to come into effect until the death of the author of the deed, and that the deed was not a bounty in any respect, but a contract, the parties to which took the property. The only question was whether the creditors who were no parties to the deed, suppose it were a bounty, could enforce it, and not whether the trust was to be executed or not, but simply and only whether it could be enforced by the creditors; and he thought it could not. But the House, affirming the judgment of the Court below, held they could.

17. The instrument may be revoked at any time before it is acted upon, or at least before any engagement is entered into with the creditors to act upon it for their benefit; and it will be revoked by any disposition of the property, either by the debtor or by the trustee or agent, inconsistent with the instrument (s).

18. Although the conveyance of the property to the agent makes no difference as to the right of revocation in the debtor (t), yet the power to revoke the trust or to recall the beneficial interest of the debtor incident to the nature of this class of instruments extends to that interest only, and not to the legal estate in any real property comprised in the instrument. That

(s) *Williams* v. *Everett*, 14 East, 582; *Scott* v. *Porcher*, 3 Mer. 662; *Garrard* v. *Lord Lauderdale*, 2 Russ. & M. 451, 456.
(t) *Mackinnon* v. *Stewart*, 1 Sim. N. S. 80, 89.

estate can be divested out of the trustees by only an express power of revocation, or a reconveyance by them of the property to the debtor, and they can rarely be advised to make such a reconveyance without the direction of a court of equity (*u*). Even where such a power is reserved to two or more of the makers of the instrument jointly and one of them dies, the power is gone; and if any trust have been created in favour of any creditor, and subject to such power, the trust would then become absolute (*x*).

19. These decisions are consistent with and do not impugn (*y*) the authority of those which establish the validity of trusts created by a voluntary settlement as against the settlor himself (*z*), or of those decisions which in other cases (*a*), and even in some cases of the nature of those the subject of the present chapter (*b*), give, or seem to give, rights to a stranger through a contract to which he is no party. The respective classes of cases rest on distinct principles.

(*u*) See *Acton* v. *Woodgate*, 2 Myl. & K. 494; *Wilding* v. *Richards*, 1 Coll. 655.

(*x*) *Montefiore* v. *Browne*, 7 H. L. C. 241.

(*y*) 3 Sim. 12; *Garrard* v. *Lord Lauderdale*, 2 Russ. & M. 451; *Bill* v. *Cureton*, 2 Myl. & K. 503, 511.

(*z*) As in *Smith* v. *Garland*, 2 Mer. 123; *Fortescue* v. *Barnett*, 3 Myl. & K. 36; *Bill* v. *Cureton; Ellison* v. *Ellison*, 6 Ves. 656; *Pulvertoft* v. *Pulvertoft*, 18 Ib. 84; *Ex parte Pye*, Ib. 140; *Paterson* v. *Murphy*, 11 Hare, 88.

(*a*) See *Taylor* v. *Stibbert*, 2 Ves. jun. 437; *Gray* v. *Knox*, 5 Ir. Eq. Rep. 451; *Stoughton* v. *Crosbie*, Ib. 465; *Steel* v. *Murphy*, 3 Ib. 1; *Marquis of Donegal* v. *Grey*, 13 Ib. 12.

(*b*) *Synnot* v. *Simpson*, 5 H. L. C. 121; *Montefiore* v. *Browne*, 7 Ib. 241.

20. Although, however, the deed may have no effect as respects the creditors, yet the trustee or agent will be allowed all payments by him in the proper execution of the trust or agency (c), and such estate as becomes vested in him by means of the deed, or by any other instrument, as a surrender of copyholds which may be connected with the deed, will not be taken from him until he has been relieved from obligations which he may have incurred on account of the debtor (d).

21. In some of the cases which are referred to in this chapter, the creditors generally or the class of creditors contemplated were expressed to be parties to the instrument, and in others of the cases they were not so expressed, but, as also in the case of creditors specifically named, merely mentioned without being recognized in terms as parties. This circumstance however did not in any way vary the application of the principle in any of these cases.

22. Whether where an instrument of the nature of those which are the subject of this chapter and revocable is also of the nature of those which are the subject of the next chapter and therefore so far irrevocable, is not irrevocable in its entirety will be noticed in the next chapter.

(c) *Wilding* v. *Richards*, 1 Coll. 655. See also *Synnot* v. *Simpson*, 5 H. L. C. 121.
(d) *Wilding* v. *Richards*; *Drever* v. *Mawdesley*, 16 Sim. 511.

CHAPTER III.

OF INSTRUMENTS FOR THE PAYMENT OF DEBTS MADE WITH THE PRIVITY OF, OR ON COMMUNICATION WITH, THE CREDITORS.

1. *Voluntary Conveyances.*
2. *Instruments for the Payment of Debts distinguishable from such Conveyances.*
3. *The Instruments considered here and those in the last Chapter differ, and how the privity of, or the communication with, the Creditors appears.*
4. *When made to a Creditor.*
5. *When so made but not for securing a Debt.*
6. *When the Creditors should come in and execute the Instrument.*
7. *Debtor covenanting to surrender, but not surrendering a Trustee.*
8. *Instruments made by way of Security.*
9. *With an express Power of Revocation.*
10. *One Creditor may sue for all.*
11. *Instruments irrevocable in part, and revocable in other part if in a separate Instrument, whether irrevocable in toto.*

1. IN equity the principle that a voluntary conveyance of property to trustees upon trust for a third party, where the trust is executed as distinguished from a trust merely executory, may create an indefeasible trust in favour of that party, is firmly established (*a*).

2. The instruments which are the subject of this chapter are distinguishable from these voluntary conveyances. These instruments, so far as they are the un-

(*a*) See cases, note (*c*), *ante*, p. 8.

solicited act, and emanating from the mere will, of the debtor alone, and even as regards consideration, as between him and the trustee, when the latter is not himself a creditor, are voluntary (*b*). And so far as they create a trust in favour of the creditors (*c*) that trust is indefeasible; but as between the debtor and his creditors, subject of course to certain statutory rights and remedies, they are not voluntary, but are founded on valuable consideration, namely, the debts themselves, and, in most cases, also the forbearance by the creditors to sue for them; for it is clear that an antecedent debt may form a valuable consideration for a distinct subsequent transaction, although nothing new proceeds from the creditor (*d*).

3. Instruments of the nature of those which are the subject of this chapter, obviously differ from those which are the subject of the last chapter. The privity of, or the communication with, the creditors commonly appears by the fact of their being made parties to and executing the instrument, or by their acts with reference to and in connection with it; and when they are parties the presumption is that the instrument was intended to create in their favour a trust which they therefore are entitled to call on the trustee to execute (*e*). For the purpose of suing upon the instrument they may become parties by being either named

(*b*) *Garrard* v. *Lord Lauderdale*, 2 Russ. & M. 451, 456.
(*c*) *Squire* v. *Ford*, 9 Hare, 47.
(*d*) *Wilding* v. *Richards*, 1 Coll. 661; *Griffith* v. *Ricketts*, 7 Hare, 299.
(*e*) See *Synnot* v. *Simpson*, 5 H. L. C. 121, 138; *Gurney* v. *Lord Oranmore*, 4 Ir. Ch. Rep. 470; on App. to D. P. *nom. Montefiore* v. *Browne*, 7 H. L. C. 241.

or described in it (*f*). The execution of the instrument however by the creditors makes them clearly parties to it, and creates between them and the trustee or agent the relation of trustee and *cestui que trust* (*g*). They may indeed take the benefit of a trust created for them without even being parties to the instrument (*h*); and under deeds executed after the 31st day of December, 1844, any person, not a party to any deed, may take an immediate benefit under it (*i*). This enactment however has been repealed as from the 1st day of October, 1845, and now under deeds executed after that day an immediate estate or interest in, and the benefit of a condition or covenant respecting, any tenements or hereditaments may be taken, although the taker be not named a party to the deed (*j*). In *Montefiore* v. *Browne* the creditor was a party to and executed the deed, which contained an express power of revocation for the debtors jointly, and by the death of one of them the power having ceased, the trust became irrevocable.

Where a creditor is a party to a deed whereby his debtor conveys property to a trustee to be applied in liquidation of the debt due to that creditor, the deed is, as to the creditor, irrevocable. A valid trust is created in his favour; and the relation between the debtor and trustee, is no longer that of mere principal

---

(*f*) *Gresty* v. *Gibson*, 4 H. & C. 28; *Reeves* v. *Watts*, 7 B. & S. 523.

(*g*) *Garrard* v. *Lord Lauderdale*, 3 Sim. 1; *Mackinnon* v. *Stewart*, 1 Sim. N. S. 76; *Lancaster* v. *Elce*, 31 Beav. 325.

(*h*) 2 Pres. Conv. 394.

(*i*) 7 & 8 Vict. c. 76, s. 11.

(*j*) 8 & 9 Vict. c. 106, ss. 1, 5.

and agent. Of course, that which is true where a single creditor is the *cestui que trust,* is at least equally so where there are many creditors. Nor does the creditor executing the deed become less a *cestui que'trust* because he gives nothing to the debtor as a consideration for the trust created in his favour, or because it was the voluntary unsolicited act of the debtor to create the trust. And where the creditors have actually executed the deed, there is no longer any possibility of treating it as a mere voluntary deed of agency revocable by the debtor (*k*).

4. These instruments are frequently made to a creditor as a trustee for the purposes of it, and such creditor then has a beneficial interest, and cannot be considered as a mere mandatory within the rule as to revocation as laid down by Lord Eldon in *Wallwyn* v. *Coutts,* and referred to by Sir L. Shadwell in *Garrard* v. *Lord Lauderdale* as the foundation of his decision. A court of law has in one case refused to extend the principle by applying it to a case where the party taking the legal interest under the deed had also a beneficial interest. In such a case it seems impossible to treat him as a mere mandatory. No assent of any third party as a creditor to come in under the deed can be necessary to perfect his title; and he seems to have a right to claim directly under the deed as a party taking a legal and equitable interest, and not as a mere mandatory who must obey the directions and is subject to the revocation of the orders of his principal. In

(*k*) *Mackinnon* v. *Stewart,* 1 Sim. N. S. 80, 89, 90; *Gurney* v. *Lord Oranmore, supra.*

Acton v. *Woodgate* (*l*) the trustees were creditors: but in that case they did not choose to claim under the first deed; and they may be considered as renouncing any title under it, which they had a clear right to do. And the creditors who were held not to be necessary parties had refused to come in under that deed. The point as to the trustees being creditors was not taken in that case; and there was enough to decide the case in favour of the trustees claiming under the second deed without reference to this question. Where, therefore, the deed is made to a creditor as a trustee for himself and others, it cannot be revoked by the assignor after it is communicated to the assignee, and is not a void deed within the rule (*m*).

Where the instrument is made to a creditor, and the debtor covenants not to revoke the powers given to the trustees, and not to prevent the execution of the trusts, and, if necessary, to concur in any sale, and to make further assurance; the instrument is clearly not revocable by the mere act of the grantor as against such creditor (*n*). It was argued, that as the instrument without the covenants just noticed would make the trustees trustees or agents for the grantor, those covenants were in substance covenants by the grantor with himself, and therefore binding upon himself only so far as he might think fit. But the Court said the covenants in question were part of the deed, and the character of the deed must be determined from a view of all its provisions, including those covenants; whereas the argument fixed the character of the deed without

(*l*) 2 Myl. & K. 492.
(*m*) *Siggers* v. *Evans*, 5 Ell. & B. 367. See also *Hunt* v. *Jessel*, 28 Beav. 100; *post*, p. 31.
(*n*) *Griffith* v. *Ricketts*, 7 Hare, 299.

reference to the covenants, which were as important as any other parts of the deed in fixing its character, and were considered by the Court as showing that the deed was intended to be irrevocable (*o*).

5. The mere fact, however, of the instrument being made to a creditor will not alone give validity to the instrument; for if the purpose and object of the deed be not for the purpose of securing any debt due to him, but to compel the creditors to come to such arrangements as he in the character of trustee may propose for the benefit of the debtor, the deed, so far as its validity depends on any debt having been due to such creditor, cannot be sustained; for the law will not permit a debtor to vest his property, even in one of his creditors, for the mere purpose of protecting himself against the claims of his other creditors, and a deed executed for such a purpose cannot be otherwise than fraudulent and void against the creditors whose interests are affected by it. Such a deed, although upon the face of it for the benefit of the creditors, is in truth a deed for the benefit of the debtor; and the creditor who accepts it takes, not for his own benefit, but for the purpose of carrying out the views and objects of the debtor in fraud of his other creditors. He becomes a party to the fraud of the debtor, and being a party to the fraud cannot be in any better position than the debtor who has perpetrated it (*p*).

6. Where no time for assenting to or adopting the deed is specified, the consenting creditors ought to

(*o*) See also *Mackinnon* v. *Stewart*, 1 Sim. N. S. 80.
(*p*) *Smith* v. *Hurst*, 10 Hare, 80.

come in without delay; for it is not the nature of transactions of this sort that creditors should be allowed to come in at any time and execute the deed; and the trustee has no power to let in a creditor at any time, or in any way to affect the debtor (*q*).

7. If by the instrument the debtor covenant to surrender his copyholds he would seem to be, until the surrender of them, a trustee for the purposes of the instrument, and on his death without making a surrender, but devising his trust estates, his estate in the copyholds would be a trust estate, and they would pass under such devise.

8. Where an instrument is made to a trustee by way of securing money advanced on the making of it by a third person, or for further securing an antecedent debt to such person, the instrument is primarily one of trust and not of mere agency, and is accepted by the trustee as much for the benefit of such creditor as of the debtor, and the creditor, although not a party to nor executing the instrument, is entitled to the benefit of and may enforce the trusts contained in it in his favour, and it is not revocable by the debtor (*r*).

So where the instrument was of two parts, between the debtor of the one part and two persons as trustees of the other part, and stated that a sum of money had been advanced by a person named to the debtor, and that he was indebted to several other persons, and had agreed to transfer all his real and personal estate to the two

---

(*q*) *Field* v. *Lord Donoughmore*, 1 Dru. & War. 227, reversing the decree of Lord Plunkett, *S. C.* 2 Dru. & Wal. 630.

(*r*) *Wilding* v. *Richards*, 1 Coll. 661. See also *Synnot* v. *Simpson*, 5 H. L. C. 121.

trustees for the benefit of all his creditors, and which he transferred accordingly upon trust for conversion into money, and out of the proceeds to pay, in the first place, the sum so advanced, and then to pay the costs of executing the trusts and then the other debts of the debtor, the Court considered it too clear for argument that the instrument was not absolutely revocable by the mere act of the debtor as against the person making such advance. In other words, that the relation of trustee and *cestui que trust* had been created between the trustees and such person (*s*).

9. Where a trust is created for the creditors, it may still be subject to an express power of revocation reserved to the debtor, and the creditor is then considered as accepting the trust as subject to such power; but when the power is reserved to two or more persons jointly, it is, on the death of one of them, gone, and the trust becomes irrevocable *t*).

10. When the instrument is made for the payment of debts generally, or of a class of debts, any creditor entitled to the benefit of the instrument of this description may sue in equity on behalf of himself and the other creditors (*u*).

11. When the instrument of the nature of those which are the subject of this chapter, and so far, if of that nature only, irrevocable, is also of the nature of those which are the subject of the second chapter, and

(*s*) *Griffith* v. *Ricketts*, 7 Hare, 299.
(*t*) *Montefiore* v. *Browne*, 7 H. L. C. 241.
(*u*) *Squire* v. *Ford*, 9 Hare, 47; *Synnot* v. *Simpson*, 5 H. L. C. 121.

so far, if of this nature only, revocable, is not irrevocable altogether, has not been decided. Contracts founded on valuable consideration containing provisions for the payment of debts, and made without the privity of the creditors, and which provisions in an instrument having no other object but such payment would be within the principles applicable to those instruments which are the subject of the second chapter, and therefore revocable, may have the effect of giving to the creditors such a right in equity as will enable them to enforce their claims against the property the subject of the contract, by means of such provisions (x). In *Acton* v. *Woodgate* (y), the first deed was made to the trustees, who were also creditors of the grantor (z), for raising and paying their own debts, and also his debts generally. By a subsequent deed, to which the debtor and the same trustees, and also certain other specified creditors, were parties, the trusts of the former deed were varied by making the trust to pay the trustees their own debts, and then to pay all other debts due from him at the time of the execution of the former deed, with certain specific exceptions; so that the position of the trustees as to their own debts was not altered. None of the general creditors were parties or privy to the first deed; but the relation of trustee and *cestui que trust* between the trustees and the specified creditors in the second deed was created by that deed, and, as to those creditors, the two deeds together were of the nature of those instruments which are the sub-

(x) See *Synnot* v. *Simpson*, 5 H. L. C. 121; *Montefiore* v. *Browne*, 7 Ib. 241.
(y) 2 Myl. & K. 492.
(z) *Vide* Chap. III.

ject of this chapter, but as to the creditors generally were of the nature of those instruments which are the subject of the second chapter. The second deed seems to have been made with the privity of, or to have been communicated to, some of the general creditors of the grantor, and thus far became of the nature of those instruments which are the subject of this chapter; for the suit was by one of such creditors against the trustees for carrying the trusts of the second deed into execution, and the court decreed accordingly; and unless there was such privity or communication the plaintiff could not, according to *Wallwyn* v. *Coutts* and the cases following it, maintain such suit. The right of such creditor, however, to maintain the suit was admitted, or at least was not questioned.

The question arose in *Griffith* v. *Ricketts* (*a*), but was not decided, although the Court seems to have been of opinion that the deed in that case was irrevocable altogether. The intention seemed to require, that inasmuch as regarded one of the trustees to whom the deed was made, who was also a creditor, and also as regarded another creditor specifically named, as to whom, however, it might be considered as in the nature of a security for a sum of money advanced by him to the debtor (*b*), the deed was irrevocable, it should be irrevocable in its entirety, at least so far as it was revocable, as soon as it had been communicated to, or acted upon by, one or more of the general creditors of the grantor.

(*a*) 7 Hare, 299.
(*b*) See also *Wilding* v. *Richards*, 1 Coll. 660.

CHAPTER IV.

OF INSTRUMENTS FOR THE PAYMENT OF DEBTS MADE WITHOUT THE PRIVITY OF, BUT AFTERWARDS COMMUNICATED TO, AND ASSENTED TO OR ADOPTED BY, THE CREDITORS.

INSTRUMENTS of the nature of those considered in the second chapter may, by the communication of them to, or by the assent to and adoption of them by, the creditors, be deprived of their mere mandatory and revocable character and quality, and become of the nature of, and within all the principles applicable to, those instruments considered in the last chapter.

SECTION I.

Of the communication of the Instrument to, or the adoption of or the assent to it by, the Creditors.

1. *Questions as to Creditors not executing, but apprized of the Execution of the Instrument, becoming* cestuis *que trust.*
2. *Execution of the Instrument by the Creditors not necessary.*
3. *What necessary to give Creditors the benefit of the Instrument.*
4. *Notice of it by the Debtor to the Creditor.*
5. *Whether the mere communication of it to the Creditors be sufficient to give them the benefit of it.*
6. *Creditor a Party to and executing the Deed.*

7. *Communication of it to be charged in Bill.*
8. *Instrument made without the privity of, and not afterwards communicated to or adopted by, the Creditors,* Synnot *v.* Simpson.

1. Where the creditors have not executed the instrument, questions have often arisen how far, by having been apprized of its execution, and so, perhaps, been induced to do, or abstain from doing, something which may affect their interests, they may not have acquired the rights of *cestuis que trust* (a).

2. It is not absolutely necessary that the creditor should execute the deed; if he assent to it, if he acquiesce in it, or act under its provisions and comply with its terms, and the other side express no dissatisfaction, he would be entitled to its benefits. The mere fact of his signature is not actually required (b).

3. Although where an order to pay a sum out of a particular fund in the hands of a third party is made the consent of such party to pay is not necessary (c), yet, as in those cases establishing the principle upon which the decisions on instruments of the nature of those considered in the second chapter rest, some communication, either by the debtor or by the agent, must be made to the person intended to be benefited to give

(a) *Mackinnon* v. *Stewart*, 1 Sim. N. S. 80, 88.
(b) *Field* v. *Lord Donoughmore*, 1 Dru. & War. 227; *Lane* v. *Husband*, 14 Sim. 656; *Evans* v. *Bagwell*, 2 Con. & L. 612; *Harland* v. *Binks*, 15 Q. B. 713; *Spottiswoode* v. *Stockdale*, Coop. 102.
(c) *Rowe* v. *Dawson*, 1 Ves. sen. 331; *Ex parte South*, 3 Swanst. 392; *Morrell* v. *Wootten*, 16 Beav. 197.

such person a legal claim against the agent (*d*), so, where an instrument containing provisions for the payment of the debts of the maker is made without the privity of his creditors, there must be some act or conduct on the part of either the grantor or the trustee or agent subsequent to the making of the deed (*e*), some distinct act of dealing with the creditors (*f*), in order to render the property comprised in, or to be affected by, the instrument liable to the demands of the creditors and to entitle them to enforce it.

4. If the debtor give to the creditors notice of the existence of the deed, and expressly or impliedly tell them that they may look to the trust property for payment of their demands, they may thereby become *cestuis que trust*, and may acquire a right as such, just as if they had been parties to and had executed the deed (*g*). It is a strong circumstance to show acquiescence in the arrangement on the part of a creditor that he is told of the deed and forbears to assert his right as a creditor: the fact of allowing six years to elapse is in favour of the creditors; they do not interfere because they are content to abide by the deed (*h*).

(*d*) *Williams* v. *Everett*, 14 East, 598; *Grant* v. *Austen*, 3 Pri. 58; *Yates* v. *Bell*, 3 B. & Ald. 643; *Wedlake* v. *Hurley*, 1 C. & J. 83; *Scott* v. *Porcher*, 3 Mer. 652; *Fitzgerald* v. *Stewart*, 2 R. & M. 457; *Lett* v. *Morris*, 4 Sim. 607; *Kirwan* v. *Daniel*, 5 Hare, 493; *Morrell* v. *Wootten*, 16 Beav. 197.

(*e*) *Cornthwaite* v. *Frith*, 4 De G. & S. 550; *Synnot* v. *Simpson*, 5 H. L. C. 121.

(*f*) *Garrard* v. *Lord Lauderdale*, 3 Sim. 1; *La Touche* v. *Lord Lucan*, 7 Cl. & F. 772; 5 H. L. C. 149; *Cosser* v. *Radford*, 1 De G. J. & S. 585.

(*g*) *Synnot* v. *Simpson*, 5 H. L. C. 121, 138; *Evans* v. *Bagwell*, 2 Con. & L. 612.

(*h*) See *Nicholson* v. *Tutin*, 2 K. & J. 18.

5. Whether the mere communication of the instrument to the creditors be sufficient to give to them the benefit of it without their assent is not quite clear. The weight of authority, however, is in the affirmative. In *Garrard* v. *Lord Lauderdale* (*i*), Shadwell, V.-C., seems to have been of opinion that such communication without the creditors ever submitting to take the benefit of the instrument, or conforming to its terms, or abstaining from suing the debtor, would be insufficient. But this was a mere dictum and not necessary for the decision of the case (*j*); and in a much later case (*k*) he seems to have entertained a contrary opinion; and the cases of *Acton* v. *Woodgate* (*l*), *Wilding* v. *Richards* (*m*), and *Griffith* v. *Ricketts* (*n*), would seem to show that such communication would be sufficient to deprive the instrument of its mandatory and revocable character, and give to those creditors to whom it is communicated the benefit of it, because they, being aware of it, might be thereby induced to a forbearance in respect of their claims which they would not otherwise have exercised (*o*). In *Browne* v. *Cavendish* (*p*), Lord St. Leonards expressed his concurrence in this opinion; adding, however, that he did not mean to bind himself to hold that, in every case, a representation to a creditor will give

(*i*) 3 Sim. 1.
(*j*) 5 Ell. & B. 377.
(*k*) *Mackinnon* v. *Stewart*, 1 Sim. N. S. 80.
(*l*) 2 M. & K. 492.
(*m*) 1 Coll. 661.
(*n*) 7 Hare, 279.
(*o*) 2 Myl. & K. 495. See also *Montefiore* v. *Browne*, 7 H. L. C. 241.
(*p*) 1 Jo. & Lat. 606, 635.

him the benefit of the trust; and that it must depend on the character of the representation and the manner it is acted on. On the other hand, he said he should be sorry to have it understood that a man may create a trust for the benefit of his creditors, communicate it to them, obtain from them the benefit of their lying by until perhaps the legal right to sue was lost, and then insist that the trust was wholly within his own power (*q*).

An instrument was made between the debtor of the one part and two other persons as trustees of the other part, and by which the debtor transferred all his estates, real and personal, to them to convert into money, and after paying a specific sum advanced to the debtor on the making of the instrument, and the costs of executing the trusts, to pay all the other debts of the debtor, and, that the instrument was not absolutely revocable by the debtor as against his creditors, between whom and the trustees such communications had taken place as would give them an interest under it, the Court held to be too clear for argument (*r*).

In *Garrard* v. *Lord Lauderdale*, Shadwell, V.-C., seems to have thought that if the creditors had received the letter which there had been sent to them, they would not have had any right to enforce the deed, inasmuch as they did not, by signing and sealing the deed, make themselves parties to it. The case to this extent, said Wigram, V.-C. (*s*), was a case of the first impression; and the decision was certainly a surprise on those in whose favour it was pronounced. The argument

(*q*) *Browne* v. *Cavendish*, 1 Jo. & Lat. 606, 635.
(*r*) *Griffith* v. *Ricketts*, 7 Hare, 299.
(*s*) *Kirwan* v. *Daniel*, 5 Hare, 493.

was that the deed, *per se*, gave no interest to the creditors; and if that were admitted then it was said a simple notice to the creditor of a deed which, *per se*, gave him no interest, could not enlarge the effect of the deed. That, said the same judge, may be true, so far as the effect of the deed is concerned; but the argument omits the material consideration, that, although the notice may not alter the effect of the deed, it may alter the position of the creditor; and Courts, both of law and equity, have repeatedly decided, that, where a creditor on whose behalf a stake has been deposited by the debtor with a third person receives notice of that fact from the stakeholder, the notice will convert the stakeholder into an agent for, and a debtor to, that creditor; and those cases have been decided on the ground that the creditor may, on the faith of the notice, have forborne to sue. The cases at law (*t*) are very strong and, in principle, not distinguishable from a trust in equity. In *Montefiore* v. *Browne* (*u*), Lord Cranworth, C., however, said: "In some of the cases it has been held, that if the existence of the trust has been communicated to the creditor, the deed is no longer revocable (*x*). Whether that is correct without considerable qualification I need not discuss." In *Smith* v. *Keating* (*y*) Parke, B., seems to have doubted whether the mere communication of the instrument to the creditors

(*t*) *Supra*, p. 8, n. (*b*); *Lilly* v. *Hays*, 5 Ad. & E. 548; *Hutchinson* v. *Heyworth*, 9 Ib. 375; *Harland* v. *Binks*, 15 Q. B. 713.

(*u*) 7 H. L. C. 241, 266.

(*x*) *Acton* v. *Woodgate*, 2 Myl. & K. 492.

(*y*) 6 C. B. 186, in Cam. Scacc.

would be sufficient. But in *Siggers* v. *Evans* (*z*) the Court of Queen's Bench seems to have been of opinion that a communication to, without an express assent by, the creditors would be sufficient to give them the benefits of the instrument.

6. Where a creditor is a party to and executes the deed, and is thereby declared a trustee of a sum to be raised under the deed for another party, the case is much stronger than where the creditor has merely notice given him of the existence of the trust, because as a party to the deed he must be assumed to have become acquainted with the contents of it, and to confine the knowledge which he acquired by the execution to the character in which he executed would be a refinement which ought not to prevail. The knowledge that the debt was satisfactorily secured would probably induce him to forbear to exercise his power of compelling payment, and thus the debtor obtains all the benefit of his creditor's forbearance by means of the trust which he thus created (*a*).

7. In order to raise an equity on a communication of the deed to the creditors, the communication must be charged in the bill (*b*).

8. An instrument, however, made even without the privity of, and not afterwards communicated to, or assented to or adopted by, the creditors, may yet be one of trust in their favour, and which they may en-

(*z*) 5 Ell. & B. 367.
(*a*) *Montefiore* v. *Browne*, 7 H. L. C. 241.
(*b*) *Per* Lord St. Leonards, *Synnot* v. *Simpson*, 5 H. L. C. 121, 130.

force against the persons claiming under the debtor the estates charged by it with the debts. Thus a father and son on the marriage of the latter settled certain estates, and as part of the contract the father conveyed to trustees a certain other estate, in trust to pay head rents, &c., and the interest of certain debts due by him and specified in a schedule to the deed, and subject to that trust, in trust for him for life, and after his death for his son absolutely. This estate thus conveyed was to be subject to the debts so specified, and the debts were to be liens and charges on it in exoneration of certain other premises, and there was a declaration that the lands vested in the trustees for payment of debts might, notwithstanding any of the trusts, be sold by the trustees for the payment of the debts and incumbrances then charged thereon with the desire and consent of the father or of the son, or the survivor. The father afterwards made another deed appointing other trustees, and with other provisions for carrying the former one into effect, and adding considerable charges to the estate so charged with debts. The trustees never interfered, none of the creditors whose debts were specified in the schedule were parties to the deed, and no notice of the deed was given to any of them, but the son paid interest on the debts according to the former deed, and he and his son wrote to creditors offering to pay them off unless they would accept a lower rate of interest. The settlor died leaving all his real and personal estates to his son absolutely, who afterwards died leaving all his real and personal estates to his son absolutely, and shortly afterwards one of the creditors scheduled sued the grandson and other persons, praying that his debts might be declared to be well charged by the indenture and schedule on the lands therein mentioned, and for an account and sale; and Brady, L. C., held that the debts were within the trusts contained in the indenture for the payment of the scheduled debts, that the son took the trust premises comprised in that indenture upon the trusts therein stated, and amongst others subject to the payment of the interest to accrue on the debts, and that the interest due and to accrue were respectively well charged by the said indenture on the trust lands; and on appeal to the House of Lords, the decree, Lord St. Leonards *dissentiente*, was affirmed. Lord Cranworth, C., was of opinion that, independently of all considerations arising from notice and conduct, the title of the respondent, the creditor, as a *cestui que trust*, was good, and that the creditors were as much the objects of the settlor's bounty as his son was, who took the estate subject to the debts, and that the trust for payment of the debts was, during the life of the settlor, a trust which he might vary or revoke at his pleasure; still, when such revocation became by his death impossible, his son could only take the estate as it was given to him, that is, subject to the scheduled debts, which according to the express provision of the deed were to be liens and charges thereon. Lord St. Leonards expressed his fear that the case would entirely unsettle the law on this subject, and said the law upon this subject was perfectly well known; and although he followed the decisions very reluctantly, yet they proceed upon a principle which, being carried out, every man can understand. He also expressed his belief that it would be found exceedingly difficult to understand, in any complicated case, whether the rule does apply or not. But as Lord Cranworth, C., said he did not dispute any of the cases, the decision must be considered as standing by itself, and does not overrule the former authorities (*c*).

Section II.

How and when the assent to, or the adoption of, the Instrument may be signified.

1. *Assent, what.*
2. *Assent by the Persons named as Trustees.*
3. *Assent or adoption by the Creditors.*
4, 5. *By the Creditors acting on the Instrument.*
6. *Receipt of Interest by them from the Debtors.*
7. *Assent, when to be given.*
8. *Creditors assenting within a time limited, whether affected by those assenting afterwards.*
9. *Assent after the death of the Debtor, when ineffectual.*
10. *Refusal not retracted.*
11. *Whether assent implied after withdrawal of express dissent.*
12. *The object of these Instruments, and how the benefits of them may be lost.*
13. *Creditor after Notice seeking payment of his Debt from another source, or not retracting a refusal.*

1. "Assent" is an ambiguous word: it may mean an external act, or a resolution of the mind (*d*). An assent may be either express or implied (*e*); but in

(*c*) *Synnot* v. *Simpson*, 5 H. L. C. 121.
(*d*) Per Erle, J., *Siggers* v. *Evans*, 5 Ell. & B. 367, 374.
(*e*) *Williams* v. *Everett*, 14 East, 598; *Fitzgerald* v. *Stewart*, 2 R. & M. 457; *Kirwan* v. *Daniel*, 5 Hare, 493; *Harland* v. *Binks*, 15 Q. B. 713.

general, an implied assent cannot be raised against an express dissent (*f*).

2. The assent of the persons named in the instrument as trustees, at least where they are also creditors, is to be presumed, although the intended trusts are "onerous trusts" (*g*). An implied assent by them, however, cannot be raised against an express dissent (*h*). If any one or more of several of such persons dissent the property will vest in the other or others (*i*).

3. A verbal assent by the creditors to the deed is sufficient. Thus where a creditor, after an explanation of the transaction to him, expressed himself as "satisfied," he was held to be assenting to the deed, so as to create privity or the relation of trustee and *cestui que trust* between him and the person to whom the deed was made (*j*). Wightman, J., said that it was not necessary to render the deed valid that some creditor must have irrevocably bound himself to come in under the deed; but that it is sufficient if any creditors have been put in such a position that their rights may have been altered, and that when they have been put in such a position the trustee cannot retire, and the deed is not revocable; at least not without the consent of those creditors whose rights may have been affected, and an option given to them to come in or decline doing so. The communications to the creditors by the trustee may have altered their position. They may

(*f*) See *Williams* v. *Everett, supra.*
(*g*) *Siggers* v. *Evans,* 5 Ell. & B. 367.
(*h*) See *Williams* v. *Everett, supra.*
(*i*) *Small* v. *Marwood,* 9 B. & C. 300, and cases cited.
(*j*) *Harland* v. *Binks,* 15 Q. B. 713.

have expressed themselves satisfied with the arrangement, and may in consequence have refrained from pursuing their legal remedies. In *Siggers* v. *Evans* (*j*), the Court seems to have been of the same opinion.

4. If the creditors act upon the deed it becomes binding, and creates a trust in their favour which they can enforce (*k*).

5. Where the trust in a deed of inspectorship was to distribute the surplus among the creditors who should become parties to and execute the deed, " or should otherwise accede to the terms thereof," Lord Cranworth, C., said that a party may bind himself by the terms of such a deed, even if there had not been the latter words, without executing it. But no person can be considered to have impliedly acceded to such a deed within the true meaning of that expression who has not put himself in precisely the same situation with regard to the debtors as if he had executed it; the principle of the rule being that if you put yourself in the situation of having the benefit of a deed you must bear its obligations, although you have not literally executed it (*l*).

6. The mere receipt of interest by the creditors from the debtors after the making of the deed, without any knowledge of the deed by the former, or any representations made to them in regard to any security provided for them, would not give a right to them to

(*j*) 5 Ell. & B. 367.
(*k*) *Per* Turner, L. J., *Cosser* v. *Radford*, 1 De G. J. & S. 585, 593.
(*l*) *Forbes* v. *Limond*, 4 De G. M. & G. 298, 315.

sue the trustees. Some distinct act of dealing with the creditors must take place to entitle them to enforce the trusts (*m*).

7. The instrument may, as indeed it always should (*n*), contain a provision for revoking or avoiding it in certain events, as may be intended (*o*), *e. g.*, unless all the creditors accede to (*p*) or refuse to execute it (*q*) within a given period, and then the refusal must be direct and positive, and not mere non-execution within the time limited for execution (*r*). The assent, however, in such cases, although given after the death of the debtor and although not within the specified period, has been held, in some cases, to be sufficient (*s*).

8. Whether, where the instrument is to be executed by the creditors within a time specified, those creditors who execute the deed within that time can be prejudiced by the other creditors who sign or assent to it after that time has been doubted (*t*).

(*m*) See *Synnot* v. *Simpson*, 5 H. L. C. 121, 149.
(*n*) *Lewis* v. *Jones*, 4 B. & C. 506.
(*o*) See *Dudgeon* v. *O'Connell*, 12 Ir. Eq. Rep. 566.
(*p*) *Spooner* v. *Whiston*, 8 J. B. Moore, 580.
(*q*) *Holmes* v. *Love*, 3 B. & C. 242; *Small* v. *Marwood*, 9 Ib. 300.
(*r*) *Holmes* v. *Love*, sup.; *Tatlock* v. *Smith*, 6 Bing. 339.
(*s*) *Dunch* v. *Kent*, 1 Vern. 260; *Spottiswoode* v. *Stockdale*, Coop. 102; *Broadbent* v. *Thornton*, 4 De G. & S. 65; *Nicholson* v. *Tutin*, 2 K. & J. 18. The accuracy of the report of *Spottiswoode* v. *Stockdale* has been questioned; *per* V.-C. Knight Bruce, 1 Coll. 678.
(*t*) See *Collins* v. *Reece*, 1 Coll. 675; *Williams* v. *Mostyn*, 12 W. R. 69; *Gould* v. *Robertson*, 4 De G. & S. 509.

9. When the deed is made in consideration of a licence and release by the creditors to the debtor, a creditor who did execute or assent to the deed in the lifetime of the debtor cannot insist upon participating in the benefits of the deed after his death (*x*).

10. So, where a creditor actually refuses to come in under or assent to the deed within the time limited, and does not within that time retract or withdraw his refusal (*y*), he cannot obtain the benefits of the deed.

11. Although, as we have just seen, against an express dissent an implied one cannot be raised, yet it may perhaps after an express dissent has been withdrawn, and can be raised without affecting the position of the debtor (*z*) or of the other creditors (*a*).

12. The object of these deeds is to protect the estate from being torn to pieces, and a court of equity, when called upon to effectuate them, is bound, in the first instance, to inquire whether the arrangements to protect the estate which were entered into between the debtor and his creditors have or have not been faithfully performed; and in every case where it finds any creditor to have deviated from and disturbed that arrangement it is bound to deprive him of all benefit under the deed. Therefore, if the acts of a creditor be such as are inconsistent with the deed, amounting in short to a repudiation of it, the creditor cannot after-

(*x*) *Lane* v. *Husband*, 14 Sim. 656.
(*y*) *Johnson* v. *Kershaw*, 1 De G. & S. 260.
(*z*) See *Lane* v. *Husband*, 14 Sim. 656.
(*a*) See *Johnson* v. *Kershaw*, *supra*.

wards claim the benefit of the deed. A court of equity in letting in one of a class of creditors to the benefit of the deed is bound to see that he has performed all its fair conditions. This is a necessary preliminary to the right of such a creditor to participate in the fund (*b*).

13. If after the communication of the instrument to a creditor he seek the satisfaction of his debt from another source than, and independent of, the instrument (*c*), or, having refused his assent to it, does not, within the time it limits for his assent, retract or withdraw his refusal (*d*), he will be deprived of the benefits of the instrument.

SECTION III.
The effect of the Communication, and of Assent or Adoption.

1. *Instrument revocable until communicated to or adopted by the Creditors.*
2. *After communication, assent or adoption, irrevocable.*
3. *The Trusts express and not affected by lapse of time between the Trustee and the Creditors.*
4. *Trust also in the cases furnishing the principle of the Decisions on these Instruments, but constructive or quasi only; and when and when not within the Statute of Limitations,* 21 Jac. 1, c. 16.
5. *Creditors not suing the Debtor on the faith of the Instrument protected in a suit impeaching the Instrument.*

1. The instrument, until the creditors have it communicated to them, or they agree or assent to it, is a mere

(*b*) *Field* v. *Lord Donoughmore*, 1 Dru. & War. 227.
(*c*) *Garrard* v. *Lord Lauderdale*, 3 Sim. 1.
(*d*) *Johnson* v. *Kershaw*, 1 De G. & S. 260.

revocable transfer, and consequently would be revoked by the insolvency of the grantor (*e*).

2. The instrument, when adopted or assented to by the creditors whose debts are to be paid under them, creates a trust for them, and is founded on valuable consideration; for an antecedent debt may form a valuable consideration for a distinct subsequent transaction, although nothing new proceeds from the creditor (*f*), and, as respects at least the adopting or assenting creditors, is no longer mandatory and revocable (*g*); but the relation of trustee and *cestui que trust* arises between the person to whom the deed is made and such creditors who may then enforce under the deed the payment of their debts (*h*).

3. The trusts under such instruments being express, and, after such adoption or assent, no longer revocable, are not, as between the trustee and the creditors, so long as that relation exists, affected by lapse of time (*i*).

4. In those cases which have furnished the principle of the decisions upon these deeds (*k*) the agent may be

(*e*) *Smith* v. *Keating*, 6 C. B. 186, in Cam. Scacc.
(*f*) See *Wilding* v. *Richards*, 1 Coll. 661.
(*g*) *Harland* v. *Binks*, 15 Q. B. 713.
(*h*) *Acton* v. *Woodgate*, 2 Myl. & K. 494; *Wilding* v. *Richards*, 1 Coll. 661; *Griffith* v. *Ricketts*, 7 Hare, 279. See also *Lilly* v. *Hays*, 5 Ad. & E. 548; *Walker* v. *Rostron*, 9 M. & W. 411; *Noble* v. *National Discount Co.*, 5 Ex. N. S. 225.
(*i*) *Townshend* v. *Townshend*, 1 B. C. C. 551; *Phillipo* v. *Munnings*, 2 Myl. & C. 309; *Wedderburn* v. *Wedderburn*, 2 Keen, 722; 4 Myl. & C. 41.
(*k*) *Ante*, p. 8, n. (*b*).

sued by the principal either at law or in equity for the property the subject of the agency (*l*); and in a suit in equity for an account, the Statute of Limitations (*m*) is not available for the agent against the principal (*n*). After the assent of the agent in favour of the creditor, the authority of the agent becomes irrevocable, and the relation of trustee and *cestui que trust* is created between them. The trust, however, is not express, but constructive or *quasi* only; the facts and dealings in the case sufficiently indicating the assent of the agent and raising, by implication, the inference that such relation may be fairly considered to be constituted (*o*). But although such a trust be so constituted, and the agent be also regarded as the agent of the creditor, whose remedy may be either at law or in equity (*p*), the agent, as against such creditor, may avail himself of the latter statute (*q*).

5. If creditors have abstained from suing the debtor upon the faith of the deed, and are not parties to a suit impeaching the deed as fraudulent and void, and no objection be raised at the hearing, or by the answers, upon the ground of their not having been made parties,

(*l*) See *Scott* v. *Porcher*, 3 Mer. 652.
(*m*) 21 Jac. 1, c. 16.
(*n*) *Lord Hollis' Case*, 2 Vent. 345; *Heath* v. *Henley*, 1 Ch. Ca. 20; *Sheldon* v. *Weldman*, Ib. 26; *Foley* v. *Hill*, 2 H. L. C. 28; *Smith* v. *Pococke*, 1 Drew. 197; *Teed* v. *Beere*, 3 Jur., N. S. 381; 28 L. J., Ch. 782, S. C.; *Crawford* v. *Crawford*, 1 Ir. Rep., Eq. S. 436.
(*o*) *Fitzgerald* v. *Stewart*, 2 Russ. & M. 457.
(*p*) See Cases, n. (*b*) p. 8, and n. (*d*) p. 35, *ante*.
(*q*) *Smith* v. *Clay*, 3 B. C. C. 639 n.

sufficient justice will be done to them and to the trustee or trustees by reserving their rights and directing such inquiries as may enable the Court to give the trustee or trustees any protection in respect of the claims of such creditors the trustee or trustees may be justly entitled to; and for that purpose the Court directs inquiries whether at any time or times, and when, after the execution of the deed, any communications or communication were or was had with any and which of the creditors of the debtor respecting the deed, and what was the nature, purport and effect of such communications or communication, and whether any and which of such creditors, at any time or times, and when, in any and what manner adopted or acted upon the deed (*r*).

(*r*) *Smith* v. *Hurst*, 10 Hare, 80.

INDEX.

ACQUIESCENCE OF CREDITORS, 35.

ACTING, 16. *See* AGENT; TRUSTEE.

AGENCY, 29.

AGENT, 3, 8, 12, 13.
    assenting and acting, 16.

ALLOWANCE,
    to trustee, 22.

ASSENT, 42, 43, 45, 46, 47. *See also* AGENT; TRUSTEE.

AUTHORITY,
    countermand of, 3.

CESTUI QUE TRUST, 2, 4, 10, 11, 12, 16, 26, 30, 34, 35, 49.

COMMUNICATION,
    to creditors to be charged in bill in equity, 39.

CONTRACT,
    strangers to, 18, 21.

CONVERSION, 13, 17, 18.

COPYHOLDS,
    covenant to surrender, 29.

COUNTERMAND OF AUTHORITY, 3.

CREDITORS,
    conveyances to pay, 2, 3, 4, 14, 17, 18, 19, 24, 26, 27.
    fraud on, 28.

CREDITORS—*continued.*
    not executing but assenting, 34, 43.
    communication to, 36, 37, 39.
    acting on a deed, 44.
    deprived of benefits, when, 46, 47.
    not parties to a suit impeaching deed as fraudulent, how protected, 49.

CREDITORS NOT PARTIES, 29.

CREDITORS PARTIES, 16, 22, 24, 25, 39.

DEATH OF DEBTOR, 16, 19.

DEBTOR,
    power of disposition, 2.
    when a trustee, 29.
    act or conduct of, 35.
    paying interest, 44.
    death of, 16, 19.

DEBTS,
    instruments for payment of, 2, 3, 4, 6, 8, 12, 14, 17, 18, 19, 24.

DEEDS,
    fraudulent, 15, 28, 49.
    of family arrangement, 18.

DISPOSITION,
    power of, by debtors, 2.

EQUITY,
    of trustee, 22.

FAMILY ARRANGEMENT,
    deeds of, 18.

FRAUD,
    on creditors, 28.

INSTRUMENTS,
    for payment of debts. *See* DEBTS.

INDEX.   53

INTENTION, 3, 4, 5, 32.

INTEREST,
 payment of, by debtor, 44.

LETTER,
 to creditors, 37.

NOTICE,
 of deed, 35. *See* Montefiore *v.* Brown, 7 H. L. Cas. 241.

ORDER TO PAY,
 out of particular fund, 34.

PARTIES,
 to instruments, 25.

POWER. *See* DISPOSITION; REVOCATION.

POWER OF DISPOSITION BY DEBTORS, 2.

POWER OF REVOCATION. *See* REVOCATION.

PRINCIPAL AND AGENT, 3, 10, 11, 13, 25.
 trust between, 49.

PRIVITY OF CREDITORS, 10, 13, 24, 35, 39.

PROTECTION TO TRUSTEE, 50.

REMEDY,
 by one creditor for all, 30.

REVOCATION, 6, 13, 14, 15, 16, 18, 20, 22, 30, 31, 32, 43, 45, 48.

STATUTES.
 21 Jac. 1, c. 16 (Limitation of Actions and Suits), 49.
 7 & 8 Vict. c. 76 (Transfer of Property), 25.
 8 & 9 Vict. c. 106 (to Amend Law of Real Property), 25.

STEWARD, 3.

STRANGERS TO CONTRACTS, 18, 21.

SURPLUS,
    revocation as to, 17.

TIME,
    for creditors' assent, 28, 45, 46.
    effect on express trusts, 48.

TRUST, 39.
    executed and executory, 23.
    express, 48.
    quasi, between principal and agent, 49.
                    agent and creditor, 49.

TRUSTEE, 2, 10, 11, 12, 16, 30, 35, 49. *See also* ASSENT; ALLOWANCE; EQUITY.

TRUST ESTATES, devise of, 29.

VENDOR AND PURCHASER, 6.

VOLUNTARY SETTLEMENTS, 2, 4, 11, 21, 23.

Lightning Source UK Ltd.
Milton Keynes UK
UKHW020009280821
389610UK00002B/273